My Teacher Jesus

by Ella K. Lindvall

Illustrated by Dwight Walles

MOODY PRESS
CHICAGO

This book

is for boys and girls

who belong to Jesus.

I belong to Jesus.

He is my friend.

He is my helper.

He is my teacher, too.

Teachers tell me

what I need to know.

Teachers tell me

what I need to do.

The best teacher is Jesus.

What Jesus Wants Me to Know

My teacher Jesus says

He loves me.

He loves me

because He is God.

He will always love me.

I belong to Jesus.

He says He forgives me

for the wrong things

I have done.

I belong to Jesus.

He says I have forever life.

Someday I will live

in heaven with Him.

Jesus says

I am in God's family.

My Father in heaven

takes good care of me.

Jesus says

He is with me

all the time.

He helps me

when trouble comes.

He says I have

a new "boss."

That boss is Jesus Himself.

He is in charge.

Jesus wants me to know

He has sent me a letter.

That letter is the Bible.

Jesus says

He likes to hear me

talk to Him.

That kind of talk

is called praying.

Jesus says I can do

some things extra well.

That is so that I can do

good work for Him.

Jesus wants me

to know about

that bad angel Satan.

Satan will tell me

to do wrong.

But God will help me

to do right

if I ask Him.

And that is good to know

Some Questions for You

1. Do you belong to Jesus?

2. What does Jesus

   want you to know

   about the wrong things

   you have done?

3. What does Jesus

   want you to know

   about living in heaven?

4. What does Jesus want you to know about trouble?

5. What does Jesus want you to know about your new "boss"?

6. What does Jesus want you to know about Satan?

What Jesus Wants Me to Do

My teacher Jesus

wants me to read

His letter the Bible

if I can.

I can always listen

when someone teaches the Bible.

That helps me to know

what makes Jesus happy.

I belong to Jesus.

He wants me to pray.

I will thank Him

for being good to me.

I will ask Him

to help other people

do what is right.

I will ask Him

to help me.

Jesus wants me

to think about Him.

I can learn Bible verses.

I can say them

to myself.

That will help.

He wants me to say

kind and true words.

He wants me to do

what my father and mother say.

That will make Him glad.

Sometimes I still do things I should not do. Jesus wants me to tell Him when I do something wrong. Then He will forgive me.

Jesus says

that choosing friends

is important.

I will choose friends

who belong to Him.

Jesus wants me

to get together

with others

who love Him.

That is why

I will go

to Sunday school.

Many people

still don't know

that Jesus is real.

He wants me

to tell them.

My teacher Jesus

wants me to remember

four big things:

1. He died for me.

2. He is alive again.

3. Some day

   He will come back.

4. And He loves me—

   today and always.

Some Questions for You

1. Do you belong to Jesus?

2. What does Jesus

    want you to do

    about the Bible?

3. What does Jesus

    want you to do

    about praying?

4. What does Jesus

want you to do

about obeying

Mother and Father?

5. What does Jesus

want you to do

when you do wrong?

6. What does Jesus

want you to remember?